This book belongs to:

_____

_____

Trace-A-Story

LITTLE

CINDERELLA

(Cursive Practice Book)

Created by Angela M. Foster

Originally published in the 1800s
by Brown, Taggard, & Chase.

ISBN 13 - 978-1502350046

ISBN 10 - 1502350041

CONTENTS

INTRODUCTION

Practice cursive handwriting in a new way!

The **Trace-A-Story** series publishes classic stories in traceable cursive and manuscript handwriting. This gives children extra practice in a more challenging setting and gives them a reason to complete the practice book. Every story is broken up into sections so that it's not too intimidating. One section per day is ideal, but since every person learns at different speeds, more or less can be done per day.

Story Summary: Just before little Cinderella's mother died, she told her "My child, always be good, and bear everything that occurs to you with patience; then, whatever toil and troubles you may suffer during life, happiness will be your lot in the end." After Cinderella's mother died, her father remarried an ill-tempered woman who had two daughters that were just as ill-tempered as their mother. The step-mother and her daughters treated Cinderella as a servant. When the prince puts on a ball that lasts for two nights, Cinderella's step-sisters attend leaving Cinderella behind to do housework. Little do they know that the Queen of Fairies is Cinderella's godmother who uses her magic to help Cinderella attend the ball disguised as an unknown princess. After attending the ball the first night, the prince was so taken by Cinderella that she asks her fairy godmother if she may attend the second night as well, and she does. Dancing all night with the prince, Cinderella forgets the time until the clock strikes twelve and her fairy godmother's magic starts wearing off. Cinderella flees for home and while doing so, accidentally steps out of one of her glass slippers which the prince finds. He orders his men to find the woman it belongs to and they soon find her, Cinderella. Will her step-sisters finally see how good of a person Cinderella is and beg her for forgiveness? Or will their jealousy rule and they try to destroy Cinderella's happy ending?

9

CURSIVE ALPHABET

A *a* | a *a* | B *B* | b *b* | C *C* |

c *c* | D *D* | d *d* | E *E* | e *e* |

F *F* | f *f* | G *G* | g *g* | H *H* |

h *h* | I *I* | i *i* | J *J* | j *j* | K *K* |

k *k* | L *L* | l *l* | M *M* | m *m* |

N *N* | n *n* | O *O* | o *o* | P *P* |

p *p* | Q *Q* | q *q* | R *R* | r *r* |

S *S* | s *s* | T *T* | t *t* | U *U* |

u *u* | V *V* | v *v* | W *W* |

w *w* | X *X* | x *x* | Y *Y* |

y *y* | Z *Z* | z *z*

DAY 1

LITTLE CINDERELLA

In former times, a rich man and his wife were the parents of a beautiful little daughter; but before she had arrived at womanhood, her dear mother fell sick, and seeing that death was near, she called her little child to her, and thus addressed her:

"My child, always be good, and bear everything that occurs to you with patience; then, whatever toil and troubles you may suffer during life, happiness will be your lot in the end."

After uttering these words the poor lady died, and her daughter was overwhelmed with grief at the loss of so good and kind a mother.

DAY 2

The father, too, was very unhappy; but he sought to get rid of his sorrow by marrying another wife; and he looked for some amiable lady who might be a second mother to his child, and a companion to himself. Unfortunately, his choice fell on a widow lady, of a proud and overbearing temper, who had two daughters by a former marriage, both as haughty and bad-tempered as herself.

DAY 3

Before marriage this woman had the cunning to conceal her bad qualities so well that she appeared to be very amiable; but the marriage was scarcely over when her real character showed itself. She could not endure her amiable step-daughter, with all her charming qualifications; for they only made her own daughters appear more hateful. She gave her the most degrading occupations,

and compelled her to wash
the dishes and clean the
stairs, and to sweep her own
rooms and those of her
sisters-in-law. When the poor
girl had finished her work,
she used to sit in the
chimney-corner amongst the
cinders, which made her
sisters give her the name of
"Cinderella." However, in her

shabby clothes Cinderella was ten times handsomer than her sisters, let them be ever so magnificently dressed.

DAY 4

The poor girl slept in the garret, upon a wretched straw mattress, whilst the bed-chambers of her sisters were furnished with every luxury and elegance, and provided with mirrors, in which they could survey themselves from head to foot. The amiable creature bore this ill treatment with patience, and did not venture to complain to her father, who was so completely governed by his wife that he would only have scolded her.

DAY 5

It happened that the king's son sent invitations to a ball, which was to last two nights, and to which all the great people of the land were invited, the two sisters among the rest. This delighted them extremely, and their thoughts were entirely occupied in selecting their

most becoming dresses for the
important occasion. Poor
Cinderella had now more
work to do than ever, as it
was her business to iron their
linen, and starch their
ruffles. The sisters talked of
nothing but preparations for
the ball. The eldest said, "I
shall wear my crimson-
velvet dress, and point-lace;"

and the younger, "I shall put on my usual dress-petticoat, a mantle embroidered with gold flowers, and a tiara of diamonds." They sent to engage the services of the most fashionable hairdresser. They also called Cinderella to their aid; for she had very good taste, and she offered, in the most amiable manner, to

arrange their heads herself; of which offer they were only too happy to avail themselves. Whilst so occupied, the eldest said, "Cinderella, should you like to go to the ball?"

DAY 6

"Alas!" said she, "you are ridiculing me. I am not likely to go to the ball."

ball

"You are right," replied the sister, "people would be amused to see a Cinderella there."

If Cinderella had been at all un-amiable she might have dressed their heads all away away, for such unkindness, but she returned good for evil, and did it in the best possible style.

The sisters were in such spirits they could scarcely eat for two days. All their time was spent before the looking-glass, and more than a dozen laces were broken in attempts to tighten their waists into elegant shapes.

DAY 7

At length the long-wished-for evening arrived, and

these proud misses stepped
into their carriage, and drove
away to the palace.
    Cinderella looked after the
coach as far as she could see,
and then returned to the
kitchen in tears, where, for
the first time, she bewailed
her hard and cruel lot, little
dreaming that a kind fairy
was at the same moment

watching over her. She
continued sobbing in the
chimney-corner until a rap
at the door aroused her, and
she got up to see what had
caused it. She found a little
old woman, hobbling on
crutches, who besought her to
give her some food.

"I have only part of my
own supper for you, Goody,

which is no better than a dry crust. But if you will step in and warm yourself by the fire, you can do so, and welcome."

DAY 8

"Thank you, my dear," said the old woman, in a feeble, croaking voice; and when she had hobbled in, and taken her seat by the fire, she continued, "Hey! dearee me! what are all these tears about, my child?"

And then Cinderella told her of all her griefs,—how her sisters had gone to the ball, and how she should like to have gone also.

"But you shall go," exclaimed her visitor, who was suddenly transformed

into a beautiful fairy, "or I
am not queen of the fairies,
or your godmother. Dry up
your tears, my dear
goddaughter, and do as I bid
you, and you shall have
clothes and horses finer than
any one."

DAY 9

As Cinderella had often
heard her father talk of her

godmother, and tell her that she was one of those kind fairies who protect good children, her spirits revived, and she wiped away her tears.

The fairy took Cinderella by the hand, and said, "Now, my dear, go into the garden, and fetch me a pumpkin."

Cinderella went

immediately to gather the
best she could find, and
carried it to her godmother,
though she could not guess
how this pumpkin could
make her go to the ball. Her
godmother took the pumpkin
and hollowed it out, leaving
only the rind; she then
struck it with her wand, and
the pumpkin was

immediately changed into a beautiful gilt coach. She next sent Cinderella for the mouse-trap, wherein were found six mice alive. She directed Cinderella to raise the door of the trap, and as each mouse came out she struck it with her wand, and it was immediately changed into a beautiful horse; so that she

had now six splendid grays
for her gilt coach.

DAY 10

The fairy was perplexed
how to find a coachman, but
Cinderella said, "I will go
and see if there is a rat in
the rat-trap; if there is, he
will make a capital
coachman."

"You are right," said the

godmother, "go and see."
Cinderella brought the rat-
trap, in which there were
three large rats. The fairy
selected one, on account of its
beautiful whiskers, and,
having touched it, it was
changed into a fat
coachman, with the finest
pair of whiskers that ever
were seen. She then said,

"You must now go into the garden, where you will find six lizards, behind the watering-pot; bring them to me." These were no sooner brought than the godmother changed them into six tall footmen, in handsome liveries, with cocked hats and gold-headed canes, who jumped up behind the coach just as if they had been accustomed to it all their lives.

DAY 11

The coachman and postilion having likewise taken their places, the fairy said to Cinderella, "Well, my dear girl, is not this as fine an equipage as you could desire, to go to the ball with?

Tell me, now, are you pleased with it?"

"O yes, dear godmother," replied Cinderella; and then, with a good deal of hesitation, she added, "but how can I make my appearance among so many finely-dressed people in these shabby clothes?"

"Give yourself no

uneasiness about that, my dear. The most difficult part of our task is already accomplished, and it will be hard if I cannot make your dress correspond with your coach and servants."

DAY 12

On saying this, the fairy touched Cinderella with her magic wand, and her clothes

were instantly changed into a most magnificent ball-dress, ornamented with the most costly jewels. The fairy now took from her pocket a beautiful pair of elastic glass slippers, which she caused Cinderella to put on; and when she had thus completed her work, and Cinderella stood before her, arrayed in

her beautiful clothes, the fairy
was much pleased, and
desired her to get into the
carriage with all expedition,
as the ball had already
commenced. Two of the
footmen then sprang and
opened the carriage-door, and
assisted Cinderella into it.
Her godmother, however,
before she took leave, strictly

charged her on no account
whatever to stay at the ball
after the clock had struck the
hour of midnight; and then
added that if she stopped but
a single moment beyond that
time her fine coach would
again become a gourd, her
horses mice, her footmen
lizards, and her old clothes
resume their former

appearance.

DAY 13

Cinderella promised faithfully to attend to everything that the fairy had mentioned; and then, quite overjoyed, gave the direction to the footman, who bawled out, in a loud voice, to the coachman, "To the royal palace!"

The coachman touched his prancing horses lightly with his whip, and swiftly the carriage started off, and in a short time reached the palace.

The arrival of so splendid an equipage as Cinderella's could not fail to attract general notice at the palace gates, and as it drove up to the marble portico the

servants, in great numbers, came out to see it.

DAY 14

The king's son, to whom it was announced that an unknown princess had arrived, hastened to receive her. He handed her out of the carriage, and led her to the ball-room. Immediately she entered the dancing ceased,

and the violins stopped
playing; so much was every
one struck with the extreme
beauty of the unknown
princess; and the only sound
heard was that of
admiration. The king, old as
he was, could not take his
eyes off her, and said, in a
low voice to the queen, that
he had not seen such a

beautiful person for many

years. All the ladies began

examining her dress, that

they might have similar ones

the next evening, if it was

possible to obtain equally rich

stuffs, and work-people

skilled enough to make them.

The king's son conducted her

to the most distinguished

place, and invited her to

dance. She danced with such grace that everybody was in raptures with her; and when supper was served the prince could partake of nothing, so much was he occupied in contemplating the beauty of the fair stranger.

DAY 15

Seated close to her sisters, Cinderella showed them

marked attention, and
divided with them the oranges
and citrons which the prince
had given her; all of which
surprised them greatly, as
they did not recognize her.
When Cinderella saw that
it wanted but a quarter of an
hour of midnight she left as
quickly as possible, making a
low courtesy to all the

company.

DAY 16

On reaching home she found her godmother there, thanked her for the delightful evening she had spent, and begged permission to go to the ball the following night, as the prince had desired her company. The fairy kindly granted her request, on condition that she would return before twelve. She then caused her clothes to resume their usual plainness, that her sisters might not know of her adventure.

Whilst Cinderella was occupied in relating all that had passed at the ball to her godmother, the two sisters knocked at the door, and as

she went to open it for them
the fairy disappeared. "O, how
late you are in coming
home," said Cinderella,
rubbing her eyes, as if just
awakened.

DAY 17

"If you had been at the
ball," said one of the sisters,
"you would not have been
tired; for there was there the

most beautiful princess that
ever was seen, who paid us
much attention, and gave us
oranges and citrons."

Cinderella could scarcely
contain herself for joy. She
asked the name of the
princess, but they said it was
not known, and that the
king's son was therefore
much distressed, and would

give anything he had to
know who she could be.

DAY 18

Cinderella smiled, and
said, "Was she, then, so very
beautiful? Could not I see
her? O, Javotte, do lend me
your yellow dress, that you
wear every day, that I may
go to the ball, and have a
peep at this wonderful

princess!"

"Indeed," said Javotte, "I am not so silly as to lend my dress to a wretched Cinderella like you."

Cinderella expected this refusal, and was very glad of it; for she would have been greatly embarrassed if her sister had lent her the dress.

DAY 19

The next evening the sisters again went to the ball, and Cinderella soon made her appearance, more magnificently dressed than before. The king's son was constantly at her side, saying the most agreeable things; so that Cinderella did not notice how the time

passed, and had quite forgot
her godmother's injunctions.
While she therefore thought it
was scarcely eleven o'clock,
she was startled by the first
stroke of midnight. She rose
very hastily, and fled as
lightly as a fawn, the prince
following, though he could
not overtake her. In her
flight she let one of her glass

slippers fall, which the prince picked up with the greatest care.

DAY 20

Cinderella arrived at home out of breath, without carriage or servants, in her shabby clothes, and had nothing remaining of all her former magnificence except one of her little glass slippers,

—the fellow of that she had lost.

Upon inquiry being made of the guards, at the palace gates, as to whether the princess had gone out, they replied that they had seen no one go out but a young girl, very poorly dressed, who looked more like a peasant than a fine lady.

DAY 21

When the two sisters returned from the ball Cinderella asked if they had enjoyed themselves, and if the beautiful lady had again been there. They told her that she had been there, but that when the clock struck twelve she had started off so quickly that she let one of her pretty

glass slippers fall off; that
the prince, who quickly
followed her, had picked it
up, and had done nothing
but look at it all the rest of
the evening; and that he was
evidently very much in love
with the beautiful creature to
whom it belonged, and would
spare no pains to find her.

DAY 22

This was indeed the case;
for, a few days after, the
prince caused it to be
published, with the sound of
trumpets, that he would
marry the lady whose foot
would exactly fit the slipper.
So the slipper was first
tried on by all the princesses,
then by all the duchesses,

and next by all the ladies
belonging to the court; but in
vain. It was then taken to
the two sisters, who tried
every possible way of getting
their foot into it, but without
success.

Cinderella, who was
looking at them, and now
recognized her slipper, said,
laughingly, "Let me see if it

will fit me."

DAY 23

The sisters immediately began to laugh, and to ridicule her; but the gentleman who had been appointed to try on the slipper, having looked attentively at Cinderella, and finding her very pretty, said she was quite right in her request; for he was ordered to try it on to everybody.

He desired her to sit down, and at once found that the slipper would go on her foot, without any trouble, and, indeed, fitted her like wax.

The astonishment of the sisters was very great, but still greater when Cinderella drew from her pocket the

fellow-slipper, and, to the great delight of the gentleman, placed it upon her other foot.

DAY 24

Her godmother now made her appearance, and, having touched Cinderella with her wand, she made her look even more magnificent than on either of the former occasions.

The sisters now recognized in Cinderella the beautiful person they had seen at the ball, and threw themselves at her feet, to implore forgiveness for all the ill-treatment they had shown her. Cinderella raised them up, and, embracing them, said she forgave them, with

all her heart, their
unkindness to her, and hoped
that for the future they would
be more kind in their
behavior to every one about
them. She told them she had
never forgotten the last words
of her mother, on her death-
bed.--"My child, always be
good, and bear with patience
everything that occurs to

you; then, whatever toils and troubles you may suffer during life, happiness will be your lot in the end."

DAY 25

These words now proved to be true; for, having borne unkindness and cruelty with patience ever since her father's second marriage, she was now going to be the wife of the king's son.

Cinderella then explained the visit of her godmother, the queen of the fairies; and how her magic wand had furnished her with dresses, carriages, and attendants; and how, by forgetting the good fairy's orders, she was obliged to quit the ball-room so suddenly; and how, in her haste, she lost her little glass slipper, and, for her disobedience, was deprived of all her fine clothes.

DAY 26

Cinderella being now betrothed to the prince, she was taken to the palace, dressed in all her splendor; and, being as amiable as she was beautiful, invited her

sisters to live in the palace
with her, where they were
soon married to two great
lords belonging to the court.
The prince thought
Cinderella more beautiful
than ever, and in a few
days married her. She was
most happy in the love of
her husband, the esteem of
the court, and the good-will

of all who knew her.

Made in the USA
San Bernardino, CA
09 September 2016